The winger's next trick was to perform a perfect nutmeg. He slipped the ball cheekily through another defender's legs, nipped around him to collect it again and then cut inside for goal.

'Watch out!' screamed the captain to wake up his dreamy goalie. 'He's going to shoot.'

Too late. The shot was already on its way. It wasn't hit with any special power, but the ball curled in a graceful arc towards the far corner of the goal. The keeper scrambled desperately across his line, as if chasing a loose piece of paper in the wind, but he was never going to catch it in time. The net did the job for him.

'*One-nil!*' exulted Luke, making no effort to keep any note of bias out of his commentary. '*A flash of magic from Brain and the Swifts are ahead. Some people might say it was against the run of play, but who cares? This is the cup! Anything can happen!*'

FOOTBALL FLUKES

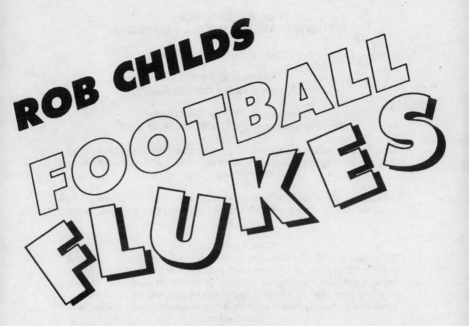

ROB CHILDS
FOOTBALL FLUKES

ILLUSTRATED BY
AIDAN POTTS

CORGI YEARLING BOOKS

FOOTBALL FLUKES
A CORGI YEARLING BOOK : 0 440 863597

First publication in Great Britain

PRINTING HISTORY
Corgi Yearling edition published 1997

Set in 12/15 pt Linotype Century Schoolbook by
Phoenix Typesetting, Ilkley, West Yorkshire

Corgi Yearling books are published by Transworld Publishers Ltd,
61–63 Uxbridge Road, Ealing, London W5 5SA,
in Australia by Transworld Publishers (Australia) Pty. Ltd,
15–25 Helles Avenue, Moorebank, NSW 2170,
and in New Zealand by Transworld Publishers (NZ) Ltd,
3 William Pickering Drive, Albany, Auckland.

Made and printed in Great Britain by
Cox & Wyman Ltd, Reading, Berkshire.

For soccer's underdogs – dream on and may your team be lucky!

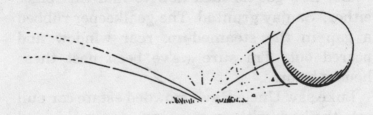

1   Cup Trail

'We're on our way to Wembley! We're on our way to Wembley! La-la-la-la! La-la-la-la!'

The hopeful chant might have carried greater conviction if dozens of travelling supporters were rocking the coach with their delirious optimism. As it was, a few off-key, croaky voices from the back of an old van didn't have quite the same effect. Even if they did belong to the actual players.

'Quit that racket, will you!' the driver ordered. 'I'm trying to concentrate on where I'm going. And it certainly isn't Wembley.'

'Are we nearly there yet, Dad?' Luke chirped up, undeterred.

Mr Crawford sighed. 'You've already asked me that twice in the last ten minutes. I'm still none the wiser. Ray's got the map.'

'Bet he's got no idea how to find this place either,' Sanjay grunted. The goalkeeper rubbed a gap in the steamed-up, rear window and peered out. 'I'm sure we've been past these houses before.'

Luke saw Uncle Ray's crowded estate car pull into the kerb without warning, causing his dad to brake suddenly and jerk his own passengers against their seat-belts. The car behind, the third member of their little football convoy, almost ran into the back of them. All three drivers got out and began a heated argument over the map in the middle of the road, involving much shaking of heads and gesticulating.

Luke consulted his watch anxiously. 'We should be there by now. It's almost kick-off time.'

'The match can't start without us, can it?' said Titch, squeezed in between Sanjay and Tubs. It was a squash even for someone as pint-sized as Titch. Tubs's vast backside took up most of the long seat.

The full-back's rumbling laugh now filled the

van too. 'I wouldn't be too sure about that. It's gonna be so one-sided, I don't suppose they'd notice whether we turned up or not.'

'Rubbish!' countered Luke vehemently. 'They'll know they've got a game on their hands once we get stuck into them. The cup's got our name on it this year, I can feel it.'

'At the rate we're going, I'd tell the engraver to make it next year, if I were you,' Sanjay observed dryly.

Luke decided it was time to take action. 'If you want a job doing properly, do it yourself,' he muttered, climbing out of the van to stop a passer-by and ask directions to the local park.

Luke did most things himself as far as his Under-13 Sunday League team were concerned. Not only was he captain of Swillsby Swifts, he was coach, trainer and player-manager too. Picking the side was the only way Luke could guarantee getting a game each week.

The three men returned sheepishly to their vehicles and the convoy trundled on – just fifty metres to the half-concealed park entrance. They were greeted, for want of a better word, by the impatient, short-tempered team manager of Digby Dynamos.

'You lot are so late, I've got every right to claim a walk-over through to the next round,' he fumed, brandishing the League's handbook at them. 'That's what the rules say in here, y'know.'

Luke's dad attempted to apologize, but the man was in no mood to listen to any excuses. He turned on his heel with a parting sneer. 'Good job for you my lads still want to play. They're out to break the club record today for the number of goals scored in a single match!'

'Right, men. All ready?' Luke demanded once the Swifts had changed.

'Ready, Skipper,' they responded dutifully, out of habit, humouring Luke's favourite rallying cry before they took the field.

'Remember, win this and we're in the last sixteen,' he beamed. 'We're on the cup trail!'

'Up a cul-de-sac, more like,' grunted Big Ben, their gangling centre-back. 'Reckon we've got more chance of winning the Lottery!'

Luke refused to tolerate any pessimism. 'You've got to be in to win. And we still are, thanks to our great victory in the first round.'

'That was a fluke and you know it. Lightning doesn't strike twice.'

'The skipper might be right for once,' Tubs cut in, making heads turn towards him in disbelief. They didn't know which notion was more weird. The idea of Luke being right, or Tubs supporting him.

13

'I mean, we *are* the strongest team in the League,' Tubs continued, struggling to keep a straight face. 'We're bottom of the table, holding everybody else up!'

'That's an old joke,' Luke retorted as Tubs's loud rumbles echoed around the bare changing room. 'League positions count for nothing in the cup. This is a one-off game. C'mon, let's get at 'em!'

The Swifts, still giggling, trotted out in their new all-gold strip with its bright green logo on the front of the shirts: GREAT GAME!

The kit was about the only thing they had won all season so far. Luke had showed off his unrivalled knowledge of football trivia in a soccer magazine competition to earn the star prize for his team. It was just a shame the Swifts weren't so hot on the pitch.

This morning, they were really caught cold. The Dynamos had been warming up for twenty minutes, increasingly annoyed at being kept waiting. Now they were like dogs suddenly let off the leash, tearing around the field, chasing and snapping at everything that moved. There seemed to be twice as many red shirts on the pitch as gold, and Luke's dad had to convince himself otherwise. He counted them to make sure.

14

Unbelievably, the Swifts' goal remained intact, adding to the home team's frustrations. Sanjay's superstitious habit before the kick-off of jumping up to touch the crossbar to bring him luck appeared for once to be working. At least, the goalkeeper thought so. Everything he missed clanged against the metal frame or flew wide of the target, as if the ball had forgotten the magic password to gain entrance into the sacred net.

Sanjay's grin broadened as another shot cannoned off his shoulder and looped up over the bar. He gave the striker a little smirk. 'Guess it's not your day, eh, pal?'

'Don't bank on it. We'll have double figures before the end.'

'Should have had them by now,' scowled the Dynamos' captain. 'C'mon, guys. Their luck can't last out much longer. Once we get the first, the floodgates will open.'

The Swifts' skipper of course didn't see it like that at all. But then Luke's rose-tinted view of the game was always different to everyone else's. As usual, he broadcast it to the world as he charged madly around after the ball, trying in vain to get a kick. It was not so much a running commentary as a stop-start, puff and pant one.

15

'Another great save by Sanjay Mistry, the Swifts' courageous custodian. He saw the ball late but got his body well behind it to concede the corner. Skipper Luke Crawford now organizes his team's marking at the set-piece, picking up the dangerous number eight himself. The ball swirls over into the goalmouth and . . . Uuuughh!'

The commentary was abruptly cut off as though someone had pulled the plug out of the socket. Luke had been flattened by the number eight's soaring leap for the ball. He felt like he'd been struck by a jumbo jet, but the impact of bodies was just enough to spoil the attacker's aim. The ball shaved a layer of rust off the outside of the upright as it zoomed by.

Not that Luke saw what happened. He was still eating dirt, face down in the six-yard box. He would have appealed for a foul if he'd had any breath left to do so. Or if he could have spat the piece of mud out of his mouth in time.

With the commentator left speechless, it was just as well that the match wasn't being televized live. The only camera on the ground was operated by Uncle Ray, roaming around the touchline. Luke liked to have the Swifts' games videoed in order to study where things had gone wrong. The analysis usually took him a very long time.

'Think I'll edit this bit out,' Luke decided, looking as if he'd just dunked his face into a vat of molten chocolate. It didn't taste like it.

Sanjay's goal was kept so much under siege that the Dynamos' keeper was relieving his boredom by leaning on a post and chatting to a couple of friends. He'd only touched the ball twice. And one of those was a hoofed clearance from a sympathetic back-pass to give him something to do.

The next time he had contact with the ball was to pick it, red-faced, out of the back of his net. Distracted by a joke, he failed to appreciate the danger when the visitors' left-winger set off on a meandering dribble. He wished now he'd left hearing the punchline till later.

Brian Draper, Brain to his teammates, was the one player of true quality that the Swifts boasted. Naturally two-footed, Brain's fancy footwork turned his baffled marker inside-out so many times that the boy's knickers must have got into the proverbial twist. Perhaps that was why he finally tripped and fell over, leaving Brain clear to torment somebody else.

The winger's next trick was to perform a perfect nutmeg. He slipped the ball cheekily through another defender's legs, nipped round

18

him to collect it again and then cut inside for goal.

'Watch out!' screamed the captain to wake up his dreamy goalie. 'He's going to shoot.'

Too late. The shot was already on its way. It wasn't hit with any special power, but the ball curled in a graceful arc towards the far corner of the goal. The keeper scrambled desperately across his line, as if chasing a loose piece of paper in the wind, but he was never going to catch it in time. The net did the job for him.

'*One-nil!*' exulted Luke, making no effort to keep any note of bias out of his commentary. '*A flash of magic from Brain and the Swifts are ahead. Some people might say it was against the run of play, but who cares? This is the cup! Anything can happen!*'

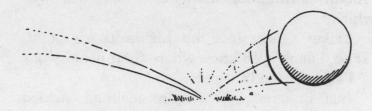

2 We Wuz Robbed!

Nobody in either camp could quite believe the 1–0 half-time scoreline.

Well, nobody except Luke. 'Told you we could win this match,' he enthused during his animated team-talk. 'We've got to hang on to this lead now. Keep a clean sheet and we're through. Concentrate on defence . . .'

The skipper was interrupted as usual. 'We've got no choice. Getting the ball over the halfway line is a major achievement.'

Luke's uncle glanced at the shirt of the speaker. Number three – Gary. Gregg wore

number ten. It was the only way he could tell the identical Garner twins apart. Their father, who had helped with transport, caught his eye and grinned. Ray smiled back, embarrassed, wondering whether Mr Garner himself had similar difficulties knowing which son was which.

Striker Gregg took up his brother's point. 'Yeah, I don't even know where their penalty box is. I've not been in it yet.'

'Just imagine how they're feeling,' cackled Sanjay. 'We've had one shot and scored. Dynamos must have had about a hundred.'

'That's football – you have to take your chances,' Luke said with a shrug. 'Right, second half. Keep it up, men. Good luck!'

'We'll need it,' laughed Gary. 'Let's hope we haven't used it all up.'

Sanjay tried to ensure that they hadn't. He was quick to repeat his 'lucky' routine, jumping up and touching the crossbar of his new goal. And this time he also blew it a kiss for good measure.

The Dynamos kicked off and their bombardment began all over again. Shots and headers rained in at Sanjay from every angle and from inside and outside the penalty area. Some went

wide, some over, some were blocked by other players or kicked off the line and scrambled away. He even managed to stop a few himself. Then, with just ten minutes to go, a shot smashed against the underside of the round, metal crossbar.

'*Oohh! What a let off!*' Luke squealed in excitement as his live commentary conveyed the full emotion of the game. *The ball ricocheted from the bar at ninety degrees, bounced up off the line and now Sanjay's safely pouched it. Dynamos are going berserk, appealing for a goal, but there's no way that went in. No way!*'

The game had to be halted. The referee was quickly surrounded by loud protesters, all insisting that they'd scored.

'C'mon, ref! That was a goal,' cried the Dynamos' captain. 'Anybody could see that.'

'Ball bounced well over the line,' claimed a teammate.

The official's indecision did little to defuse the situation. 'Sorry, I'm not sure that it did,' he faltered. 'It all happened so quickly.'

'Then ask the linesman,' the captain demanded. 'He's got his flag up. Go over and talk to him.'

There was hardly any need to do that. The linesman was making it perfectly plain what his views were. He was jumping up and down, screaming that it was a goal. The referee considered that the linesman's judgement might not exactly be neutral. He was the Dynamos' manager.

'The whole ball has to cross the line, and I can't be certain that it did,' the referee explained to the players. 'I'm giving the goalkeeper the benefit of the doubt. No goal!'

The captain went ballistic! He seemed to lose all self control and gave vent to a whole string of swear words, most of them directed at the

24

referee. Then everybody saw red: the red card that the official drew out of his top pocket and flourished at the boy.

'Off!' he ordered. 'I'm sending you off for using abusive language. You'll be reported to the League and suspended.'

The player was totally gobsmacked. 'You c-can't do that,' he stammered out. 'I'm the captain.'

'It doesn't matter if you're the Archbishop of Canterbury! I'm the ref and I'm in charge. And you're off!'

The man pointed sternly to the changing rooms and the boy's shoulders sagged. He

realized he had not only let himself down, but his side too. They were now reduced to ten men. He turned, his lips visibly quivering, and trudged off the field to the stunned silence of his team-mates. He didn't want anybody to see his tears.

The drama wasn't over yet. As the captain departed, Luke saw Uncle Ray being led by the arm across the pitch towards them by the Dynamos' manager.

'Take a look at this, ref,' the manager yelled out. 'We've got video evidence here. This'll prove it was a goal!'

'I don't even know if I got a proper shot of it,' Ray was saying, trying not to drop the camcorder into the mud. 'I haven't really got the hang of this thing yet. It's not easy, you know . . .'

'Excuses, excuses. C'mon, ref! Take a butcher's at this film.'

The referee stood firm. 'You can't expect me to stand here and squint at some fuzzy action-replay before making a decision. That's nonsense. Now if you don't get off the pitch straightaway and let the match continue, I'll abandon it in favour of the Swifts.'

The manager deflated like a pricked balloon. He went away muttering, leaving his players to sort themselves out as best they could.

'C'mon, we can still beat this lot even with half a team!' cried the Dynamos' leading scorer, taking over the captaincy.

Getting so steamed up, though, had ruined the quality of their football and the Dynamos never looked likely to break their scoring hoodoo. Against all logic, the Swifts seemed to be holding out for a shock victory, despite the generous amount of added time being allowed for the long dispute.

'Blow that whistle, ref!' pleaded Luke's dad from the touchline. 'This game's going on for ever.'

The referee obliged – but not for the desired reason. In the dying seconds, Tubs made a clumsy challenge for the ball inside the area and the winger collapsed like an imploded factory chimney. Appeals rang out from all around the pitch. The referee took a deep breath, then blew a shrill peep and pointed to the spot.

Penalty!

'The kid dived!' Tubs complained loudly.

'Not fair, ref!' Big Ben joined in. 'You've just given it to make up for all that other business.'

'Don't argue, lads,' the referee said, almost apologetically. 'You won't change my decision.'

He also made it clear that time was up. 'The

27

game's over apart from the actual penalty kick. No rebound will be allowed.'

Sanjay and the new captain tried to outstare each other while the rest of the players stood around the edge of the area. There was nothing more anybody else could do. If the penalty went in, there would have to be a replay. It all depended on this kick. Or at least they thought so.

As his opponent ran in to shoot, Sanjay decided to go to his left. It was a good guess. He dived and pulled off a fine save, parrying the well-placed drive. He didn't care where the ball

went. The goalie jumped to his feet just before he was mobbed by his jubilant teammates.

It took a while for the referee's whistle to restore some kind of order. 'Doesn't count!' he announced. 'Goalkeeper moved before the ball was struck. The penalty will have to be retaken.'

The referee suddenly went from villain to hero in the eyes of the Dynamos. They had another chance to save the game, but the Swifts felt crushed by the disappointment. The kicker respotted the ball, turned away from the goal and walked slowly back, planning what he should do.

Luke's commentary was now little more than a whispered croak as he almost choked on the tension of the moment. Most of the players didn't even dare to look.

'*So close to glory. Will triumph turn to disaster? Sanjay crouches on his line again, wondering which way to go. Will the kicker try and put it in the same place or not? It's a game of double bluff. Who's going to win this crucial psychological duel?*'

Luke's English class at school had recently been studying Rudyard Kipling's famous poem, *If.* His subconscious mention of the poet's two impostors, Triumph and Disaster, triggered off

half-remembered snatches of lines in his fertile mind:

If you can keep your head
When all about you are losing theirs . . .
You'll be a man, my son!

'Keep your head, Sanjay,' he burbled to himself in the nerve-wracking silence before the kick. 'Be a man, my son!'

The penalty-taker decided to rely on brute strength rather than placement. He blasted the ball with all his might, but Sanjay this time held his position in the centre of the goal. He didn't want to give the referee any excuse to rule out a save.

If Sanjay had dived either way, he'd have missed it. The ball came straight at him like a laser. His block was based on sheer instinct for survival, and it was just as well that his goalie's reflexes were razor sharp. If he hadn't raised his arms in front of his face in time, the cannonball would probably have knocked his head off!

As it was, Sanjay was sent tumbling backwards into the net – but the ball didn't go with him. It went spiralling away somewhere up into the air and the kicker sank to his knees in

30

despair as the Swifts ran past him to lift their saviour shoulder high. The match was won – and lost.

'You're the man, Sanjay!' Luke cried out. 'The main man.'

Their noisy celebrations continued in the changing room, in stark contrast to the deathly hush on the other side of the thin partition. Luke was the most raucous of the lot, but his dad and uncle at least made an attempt to offer their commiserations to the losers.

They were quite relieved in a sense to find the Dynamos' door closed and locked. 'Best not to disturb them, eh?' whispered Ray.

'Aye, reckon so,' nodded his elder brother. 'Hurry the lads up. We'll slip away before the Dynamos' chappie wants to see that video of yours!'

Luke of course made a special point of watching the tape as soon as he got home – in private on the portable TV set in his bedroom.

'Ah well!' he sighed after he'd reviewed the crossbar incident several times. 'I guess everybody's human. Even referees!'

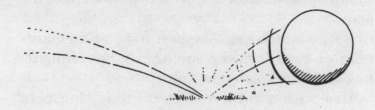

3 Football Fantasy

It was dark too early now for the Swifts to practise outdoors in midweek. Luke had them reporting for duty instead on the village recreation ground on Saturday mornings – so long as there wasn't a school match arranged.

Not that any fixture clash would have disrupted the Swifts' training plans too much. Only Sanjay and the Garner twins were regular members of the Comprehensive's Year 8 soccer team, but Luke was ever hopeful of being called up himself to play. He kept those Saturdays free.

After their epic cup victory, however, a team

get-together was a must. They all wanted to savour it further by re-living their many lucky escapes.

'Guess it was just one of those games,' said Titch, shaking his head. 'I bet the Dynamos wouldn't have scored if we'd still been playing now.'

'Better watch out, Skipper. If we go on giant-killing like this in the cup, they'll be calling us Luke's Flukes!' laughed Gary.

'Hey! Got a nice ring to it, that,' his twin grinned. 'I prefer it to Swillsby Swifts. Can we change our name mid-season, Skipper?'

Luke gave him a hard stare. 'No, we can't. Besides, it wasn't fluky. Good teams make their own luck.'

'Well how come we had so much, then?' chortled Tubs. 'We're rubbish!'

'Speak for yourself,' Sanjay cut in, smirking. 'It was you who gave away that last minute penalty, and it was me who saved it – twice!'

'OK, OK, we know,' Tubs conceded. 'But I hardly touched the guy.'

'Can't say I blame him for diving out the way,' Titch said. 'He was probably scared you'd roll on him and squash him flat.'

'I keep thinking about that great bust-up with

the ref,' said Brain. 'Did the ball really go in? I couldn't see from where I was.'

'The ref said it wasn't a goal, so it wasn't a goal,' Luke said simply. 'Rule number one of good sportsmanship: the referee is always right.'

'Even when he's wrong, Skip?' chipped in Dazza, their right-winger.

'Well, everybody makes mistakes. All teams receive their fair share of good and bad decisions over a season. You just have to accept them and get on with the game.'

Big Ben looked thoughtful for a moment, which is not easy to do when you're standing in the middle of a draughty changing cabin in your Batman boxer shorts. His long thin legs stuck out of them like a couple of cricket stumps. 'By the way, Luke, what *did* that video show?'

Luke liked to be called Skipper at Swifts' sessions, but he let Big Ben's lapse go uncorrected. He was unnaturally evasive with his response too. 'Oh, nothing worth mentioning,' he said, adding a little nervous cough. 'You know what Ray's filming is like. He's not exactly Steven Spielberg with the camera, is he?'

'So couldn't you tell?'

'Nah, the ball bounced down behind Sanjay and went out of sight.'

'I got in the way of all the shots last Sunday,' the goalie grinned.

'Not surprised with a head your size,' Tubs laughed, getting his own back for the many jibes he had to put up with from Sanjay.

'Can we watch the video of the game sometime, Skipper?' asked Brain.

'Er, no, sorry,' Luke apologized. 'It got wiped off by mistake.'

'What! You mean I won't be able to see all my saves again?' gasped Sanjay in genuine dismay. 'How did it happen?'

'Dad went and recorded *The X-Files* over it.'

'Bet even they couldn't solve this mystery!' laughed Gary. 'Was it a goal or wasn't it? Is Sanjay really an alien?'

'It's like that Geoff Hurst goal in the '66 World Cup Final at Wembley,' said Big Ben. 'Y'know, when his shot hit the bar. They're still arguing now about whether or not it bounced down over the line.'

'The linesman said it did, that's all that matters,' Titch pointed out. 'If it wasn't for him, England might not have won the World Cup.'

'Tofik Bakhramov.'

'Pardon, Skip,' said Dazza. 'You say something?'

'Yes, Tofik Bakhramov,' Luke repeated. 'That was the name of the Russian linesman that day.'

The whole cabin burst out laughing at yet another example of Luke's encyclopedic knowledge of the game's trivia. 'You're a mine of useless information,' Gregg teased him. 'I bet you even know the names of all the people in the crowd as well.'

'I know three of them,' Luke smiled. 'Philip Crawford, Ray Crawford and Harold Crawford.'

'Your dad and uncle were actually at that World Cup Final? Magic! Who's this Harold, though?'

'My grandad. He got tickets for the big match and took his kids. They were only about our age at the time. Dad still talks about seeing Hurst's hat-trick.'

That was the cue for most of them to pick up the famous commentary. *'Some people are on the pitch . . . they think it's all over – it is now!'*

Luke wished that he might come out with something equally memorable like that one day himself on TV. He'd just have to keep practising.

'Well it's all over now for the Dynamos, that's for sure,' he grinned. 'But not for us. Up the Swifts! We're gonna win the cup!'

'Dream on, Skipper,' chuckled Tubs. 'Dream on!'

. . . the cross comes over into the penalty area and there's skipper Luke Crawford on the end of it as usual. You just can't keep this boy out of the game. He controls the ball on his chest and as it drops, he smacks it fiercely on the volley with his left foot . . .

. . . the keeper has no chance of reaching it. Ohhh! The ball hits the bar and bounces down and out again. Is it a goal? Yes – no – nobody's sure. Not even the Russian linesman . . .

. . . it doesn't matter. Luke has saved the officials from having to make a controversial decision. He's reacted quicker than anybody else and met the rebound with his head, guiding the ball over the stranded keeper into the opposite corner of the net . . .

. . . what a goal! What a player! Already Luke Crawford is well into his famous goal celebration routine. He performs a sequence of acrobatic tumbles, leaps and somersaults that would surely win a gold medal in the Olympic gymnastics competition . . .

. . . that was Luke's second goal of the game, giving his team a four–nil lead. He's made the other two goals as well, but you can bet he'll want to set the seal on this Cup Final by scoring a hattrick. It'll put his name into the record books yet again . . .

. . . it doesn't take the skipper long. He wins the ball himself inside his own half and sets off on an amazing solo run, demonstrating all his dribbling skills to the cheering crowds. He's beaten one, two, three, four men so far and now the keeper's coming out to try and narrow the shooting angle. Luke has no intention of shooting. He sells the poor keeper a wicked dummy, leaving him sprawled on the grass, nips

past him and runs the ball cheekily into the empty net . . .

. . . he treats his fans to another exhibition of his acrobatics, this time taking the ball with him and juggling it up in the air at the same time. Incredible! Is there nothing this boy can't do? Many people rate him the finest footballer ever, but Luke just shakes his head. 'That honour belongs to Johan,' he always says modestly . . .

. . . and now, at the final whistle, after skippering his side to an overwhelming five–nil victory, Luke is rewarded by meeting his longtime hero. The trophy is presented to him by none other than Johan Cruyff, the legendary Flying Dutchman, the man who inspired Luke to grace the game of football with his tremendous talents . . .

. . . what an emotional scene! The two stars shake hands and embrace in mutual respect before Luke Crawford holds the silver trophy up high to huge roars from the crowd. They think it's all over – it is now. It's a dream come true . . .

'Luke! C'mon, wake up, Luke!' yelled his dad from the bottom of the stairs. 'Match day, sleepyhead. We've got to be off soon. Get up!'

Luke struggled up on to his elbow and

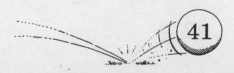

scratched his tousled mop of fair hair. The dream remained so vivid in his mind, he could still picture himself side by side with the great Johan.

'It's got to mean something,' he murmured, lost in wonder. 'Perhaps it's an omen. Perhaps the Swifts really are gonna go all the way . . .'

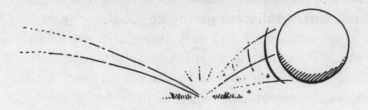

4   Misfits

After the dream came reality – the battle for precious league points.

Luke hated the thought of the Swifts being relegated in their first season. He hadn't formed the team with that possibility in mind at all. He'd set his original sights on promotion.

This was another away game, but much nearer Swillsby. One day, Luke hoped, the Swifts might roll up at some venue with a great cavalcade of cars to impress the home side with the strength of their support. It could even be worth a goal start, as they knew to their own cost.

As usual, however, they were fortunate to muster three vehicles. Instead of sweeping into the car park in a cloud of dust, they trickled almost apologetically through the gates and bumped across the field towards the changing hut with hardly anyone noticing their arrival. At least they were on time.

That was about the only thing the Swifts got right. They were outplayed, outfought and outclassed from start to finish. Their well-organized opponents were simply too good for them in every department and made the most of their superior abilities.

Sanjay let the first goal in through his legs and conceded the seventh a minute from time. Luke was back 'helping' in defence and deflected a shot that Sanjay had covered straight to the feet of an unmarked attacker.

It wasn't a matter of luck suddenly deserting them. They were lucky only to lose 7–0. It might easily have been twice that many.

'Ah well, it was nice while it lasted,' sighed Big Ben in the hut afterwards, examining a number of bruises on his legs.

'What was?' asked Gary.

'Winning. I might have got used to that, given time.'

44

'Yeah, back to normal now,' said Tubs. 'If there's one thing we're consistently good at, it's getting stuffed!'

The remark was too flippant for Luke. 'Look, we'd do a lot better if only we believed in ourselves more. Then we might surprise a few people by showing them we can play a bit.'

'It'd surprise me for a kick-off,' Tubs grunted. 'I mean, just look at us, all shapes and sizes. A bunch of misfits.'

'Hark at the blubber mountain!' Sanjay cut in.

'OK, so I'm fat,' Tubs snapped back, for once losing his sense of humour. 'Most of us are here 'cos we know nobody else would have us.'

The twins glanced at each other and almost telepathically burst into song together: *'Always look on the bright side of life!'*

'That's half the trouble,' Luke retorted. 'I wish you'd all start to take things more seriously – before it's too late. You just seem to turn up every Sunday to kick a ball about, not caring whether we win or lose.'

'I thought that was the name of the game, Skip,' said Dazza. 'Y'know, enjoying our soccer was more important than the final result.'

'Well, yes it is, but we enjoy it far more when we've won, don't we?'

'Sure,' Gary agreed, 'but no need to get too heavy. We've only lost a footie match. It's not a disaster.'

'Not like the end of the world,' added Gregg.

'I know that,' Luke insisted. 'But it might be the end of the Swifts if we drop out of the League. I mean, the squad might break up. And who'd bother to run another team in the village if I packed it in too?'

'At last some good news,' Sanjay laughed. 'The skipper's thinking of hanging up his boots!'

'Oh well, if that's the way you feel,' Luke said sadly.

'Don't take it personally, Skipper. Only joking.

47

I mean, where would we be without you?'

'Top of the league?' Gary suggested and then took cover as Luke threw a sweaty sock at him.

'Are you saying we don't try?' said Big Ben accusingly. 'Just look at my bruises. I didn't get those sunbathing in the penalty box, you know.'

'I appreciate that,' said Luke, smoothing the centre-back's ruffled feathers. 'But all of us need to practise our skills more and get fitter. And we've got to work together properly as a team to take the pressure off you people in defence for a while.'

The skipper decided to tell the others of his dream, hoping it might inspire them. He wisely left out mention of his own heroic deeds in scoring a hat-trick, but he couldn't resist the part about the cup being presented by the maestro.

His players found it impossible to stifle their giggles. 'You and your Johan,' rumbled Tubs. 'Pity he doesn't know how much you idolize him.'

'You reckon this dream of yours was a sign, then, that we might really win the cup?' said Brain.

'Why not? Somebody's got to, haven't they? Positive thinking!'

'It could be you!' intoned Gary, imitating the

Lottery's lucky finger of fate.

'Yeah, but not us,' wheezed Tubs, pulling on his marquee-sized coat. 'C'mon, time to go home. Let's leave Luke to his dreams.'

Luke sighed and consoled himself with Kipling's words:

'If you can dream, and not make dreams
your master . . .
You'll be a man, my son!'

He fully recognized that it would take more than dreams to boost the Swifts' confidence. It would take a lot of hard work – and luck. And finding one or two new players from somewhere to bolster their squad wouldn't do any harm either . . .

A small, under-strength pool of players was a problem that the Swifts shared with Swillsby Comprehensive School.

The Year 8 group in particular was a victim of falling numbers, though this was due more to the sharp tongue of their sports teacher, 'Frosty' Winter, than to any decline in the local birthrate. Several promising players had already dropped out of the soccer squad.

Luke wasn't one of them. His love of the game ensured that he hadn't missed a single school team training session. He always bounced back from Frosty's sarcastic criticisms of his abilities like a ball off a crossbar.

He also attended as many of their matches as possible. Keeping soccer statistics was his hobby and Luke had logged details of every game they'd played since he'd joined the school. Sometimes he had to rely on cousin Jon, Uncle Ray's son, for accounts of away matches, but Jon wasn't that reliable. He was the Comp's star performer and not interested in facts and figures.

If Luke was really desperate for information, he had to ask Frosty and that was even worse. Frosty's memory of who'd scored seemed even shorter than his temper, especially after a Comp defeat – a common occurrence.

The teacher knew, however, that Luke would be on hand if other players failed to show up, even though turning to such an emergency substitute was very much a last resort. The boy's previous catastrophic appearances still tended to wake him up in the middle of the night in a cold sweat.

Frosty feared that he was going to have to risk using Luke once more to make up the numbers

for their next match, a home fixture against Clevefield Comprehensive. Four of the regulars were needed for county cross-country trials on the same morning.

Fortunately, his two best players were still available: Jon Crawford and captain Matthew Clarke. But Matthew's growing disenchantment with representing the school only increased further when he saw the extra names on the team sheet.

'Not Loony Luke,' he groaned, gazing in disbelief at the sports noticeboard. 'Wish I'd gone in for the cross-country now.'

Centre-back Adam, a teammate also of Matthew and Jon for their Sunday side, Padley Panthers, was quick to agree. 'There's Big Ben and Tubs too. We've lost before we even start.'

'Yeah, and the only decent player the Sloths *have* got ain't here,' Matthew scowled, using his derogatory nickname for the Swifts. 'Brain is too scared of Frosty to come to any of the practices.'

'Think I might just stay in bed,' grunted Adam.

Frosty anxiously counted heads as the boys arrived on Saturday morning and breathed a sigh of relief when he reached twelve. Until he realized he had included Sanjay's younger brother, still at the primary school.

'Rather pick him than Luke, if I could,' Frosty murmured under his breath, resigned to his fate.

Then Adam strolled casually into the changing room. The defender was ten minutes late, but Frosty welcomed him like the prodigal son. Adam had to duck quickly away. He'd been bracing himself for the expected blast about his timekeeping and lost his cool when he thought for one horrible moment that Frosty was actually going to kiss him!

The teacher struggled to put on a serious face to break the 'bad' news to Luke. 'Sorry, it's the

subs' bench for you again,' he began, tossing him a black and white striped shirt. 'Hope you don't mind.'

It came as no surprise that he'd been lumbered with the number thirteen top as usual – Frosty's pathetic little private joke. Luke pulled it over his head straightaway, not wanting to let him have the satisfaction of seeing his disappointment.

'Funny how he can never find any other spare shirt when I'm involved,' Luke muttered. 'But I'll show him, given half a chance.'

Despite all Frosty's best endeavours, the number thirteen was soon to find himself allowed a far bigger fraction than that . . .

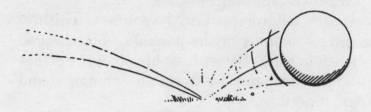

5 Frostbite

Midway through the first half, Tubs pulled up lame.

Frosty whistled the game to a halt and went across to the overweight full-back. With the Comp already 2–0 down, he was not feeling sympathetic. 'The winger's running rings round you. What's the matter?'

Tubs grimaced. 'Think I've done my groin in, sir. Felt a tweak playing for the Swifts last Sunday and now it's got worse.'

Frosty glanced round in panic towards Luke. The substitute was already warming up on the

touchline. 'Can't you carry on? How bad is it?'

'Bad, sir, sorry. It's agony!'

As Tubs hobbled from the field, Frosty reluctantly signalled his sub to come on and Luke was by his side in an instant.

'Where do you want me, sir?'

Frosty felt tempted to give him a truthful answer – as far away as possible – but checked himself in time. 'Better take his place in defence till half-time and we'll change things round then, if need be.'

Luke didn't mind where he played. The main thing was that he was on the pitch. On Sundays he gave himself licence to roam, which meant chasing after the ball wherever it went, and he found it very difficult to curb his natural instincts. He always wanted to be where the action was.

Now he forced himself deliberately to stay back in defence and mark Clevefield's left-winger. He found it a terrific strain, watching from a distance as the Comp attacked down the other side of the pitch. Even to commentate he needed binoculars.

'After the Comp's wretched start, they've now brought on their underrated utility player, Luke Crawford, to shore up the defence. If they can stop

56

*leaking goals, the team have got the quality
strikers to get them back into this game. And
here's the best of them on the ball as I speak.
Luke's multi-talented cousin Jon cuts inside
from the wing, creating the space to shoot. Will
he hit it with his right or his left? He's lethal with
both feet, just like Johan Cruyff . . .'*

'Belt up, will you!'

'Eh?' Luke was just getting into full flow when
he had to break out of commentary mode to see
who'd interrupted him. The winger was glaring
at him, but Luke was equally irritated. He
hadn't been able to describe Jon's dipping shot

that narrowly cleared the crossbar. 'What's up with you?'

'You! That's what's up. I'm not gonna put up with you droning on like that for the rest of the match – so just shut it, OK?'

'No, it's not OK,' retorted Luke and switched his imaginary microphone back on – full volume. *The Clevefield winger is obviously rattled now that he knows he's met his match with his new marker. He may not get another kick . . . Owww!'*

The boy made sure he did get another kick – on the back of Luke's legs – before nipping out the way of any possible retaliation. 'That was just a friendly warning,' he sneered. 'If you open your stupid mouth again, I'll put my boot in that instead next time.'

With the ball at the other end of the pitch, nobody had seen the incident and Luke knew there was no point in complaining to the referee. Frosty wouldn't do anything about it. He had to suffer in silence, nursing the blow to his legs and to his pride.

Luke didn't much fancy tangling physically with the tall winger. He comforted himself by imagining a notice of apology at the bottom of the screen. *We are sorry for the temporary loss of sound. The game will continue in vision only.*

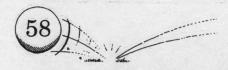

Normal service will be resumed as soon as possible, but in the meantime, here is some music . . .'

The winger looked round accusingly. There was a loud humming noise coming from somewhere, although he couldn't be quite sure who or what was making it. But he had a pretty good idea.

By the interval, the Comp were trailing 4–0 and wishing it was full time instead. It might have been even worse. Just before the whistle, Luke had saved a fifth by blocking the ball on the goal-line, allowing Sanjay to recover and dive on top of it.

'Good stop, that, Luke,' said Jon as the players trudged towards Frosty for the expected ear-bashing. 'You couldn't have been better positioned.'

Luke grinned, basking in any praise he received. It was so rare, the novelty never wore off. 'Don't suppose old Frosty will mention it.'

'Unusual style, though,' his cousin smiled, amused by the way the ball had rolled against Luke's neck. 'What were you doing lying there like that in the first place?'

'Got tripped up in the goalmouth scramble, didn't I? Probably that winger. Real head-case, he is.'

'You mean the one who's scored a hat-trick?'

Luke ignored the implied jibe at his defensive deficiencies. 'Yeah, that's the one. He keeps having a go at me. Dead vicious, like.'

Luke explained quickly what had been happening and while Jon took it seriously enough, Matthew clearly didn't. Luke could see him smirking when Jon had a quiet word with the captain about it. Adam was sniggering too, not really listening to all Frosty's criticisms.

'This is just a damage limitation exercise now,' the teacher told them. 'We've already lost this match, but we need to stop it becoming a rout.

That winger's murdering us.'

'He's certainly committing GBH on me,' Luke muttered grimly.

Frosty made wholesale positional changes for the second half, directing Adam to mark the winger. Luke was moved up on to the wing himself with instructions to hug the touchline. Out of harm's way, Frosty hoped.

Adam intended to make an immediate impact. Straight after the restart he wandered over to introduce himself to their first-half tormentor, holding out his hand. 'Congratulations!' he said with a grin.

'What d'yer mean?' the winger said, eyeing him suspiciously. They'd already clashed a couple of times in the penalty area, fouls that the referee had chosen to overlook.

'I gather you managed to shut our idiot number thirteen up. Well done, we've been trying to do that ourselves all season. How did you do it?'

The boy relaxed his guard slightly and accepted Adam's handshake. 'Well, I just . . .'

He stopped as he became aware of the pain in his right hand. Adam had also gripped his arm and now tightened the pressure. 'Hey! You're hurting me,' he complained.

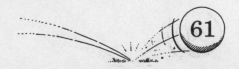

'Yeah, I know,' Adam snarled. 'If the teacher says mark somebody, I mark 'em all right. I think three goals are enough, don't you, pal?'

The winger nodded his head furiously. 'OK, OK, I get the message,' he cried. 'I'll back off.'

Adam released him as a few spectators began to show an interest in their little tête-à-tête. 'Good man, I knew you'd see my point of view. Enjoy the second half.'

That was the closest the winger got to Adam for the rest of the match. He didn't even risk shaking hands with him again after the final whistle.

With their hat-trick hero mysteriously subdued, the Clevefield attack carried little more threat. Swillsby were able to go on the offensive themselves and would have scored sooner than they did if Luke hadn't kept popping up in the unlikeliest of places. His untimely involvement disrupted all their most promising moves.

'Keep out on that wing!' Frosty growled at him. 'You're a menace. I should have given you one of their red shirts, not one of ours!'

The teacher's stinging words were like water off an ugly duckling's back to Luke. He was used to them. He was running free and enjoying himself again, unshackled by any defensive duties.

'The Comp are well on top now, despite the scoreline,' his resurrected commentary burbled happily. *'There's only one team in it this half with Luke Crawford breathing fresh life into their attack. It's only a matter of time before the goals must come. And look, here's the captain now, linking up with Jon outside the area before letting fly at goal . . . Ow! . . . Oh dear, the shot's been blocked . . . pity!'*

It was more than a pity for Matthew. Luke had failed to mention that it was the player-commen-

tator himself who had inadvertently wandered across the line of the captain's drive that was destined for the net.

Matthew's language made the Dynamos' foul-mouthed captain seem like he had a limited vocabulary. Threats and curses rained down on Luke and he took these far more seriously than Frosty's rantings. He retired to the wing and busied himself there with his commentary. He described in lavish detail not only the two goals Matthew and Jon did eventually score, but also Big Ben's comical own goal, back-heading the ball past Sanjay.

'Well, five-two, could have been worse,' Luke babbled to Jon as they trooped in to the changing rooms. 'Great goal of yours. Johan would have been proud of that one.'

His cousin gave his habitual, casual shrug, a characteristic mannerism that he'd made almost into an art form. 'Yeah, not bad, I suppose. Soz about Matt. He was out of order there, swearing at you like that.'

Luke tried to copy the shrug, but didn't quite pull it off. He mistimed his shoulders, making it look like he had a nervous tic. 'No sweat. I've got more important things to worry about than Matthew.'

'Such as?'

'Such as the injury to Tubs. Looks like he could be out of action for a while. He might have to miss our next cup match.'

'Shame. You might have a fair chance of getting through as well.'

Luke looked at him. 'How d'yer mean? We don't even know who we're playing yet.'

Jon grinned. 'Hasn't Dad told you? He got the news yesterday.'

Luke couldn't believe it. Uncle Ray was the Swifts' official team contact and received all the letters from the League Secretary before passing them to him. 'You're having me on.'

'No, straight up. You've been drawn at home – against Brenton Blues. Aren't they in the same division as you?'

Luke leapt up and punched the air in delight. 'Ye–es!' he cried out. 'We can lick them OK. Quarter-finals here we come!'

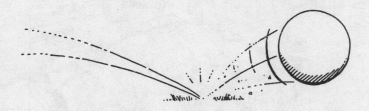

6　Tactical Changes

Sitting at the desk in his bedroom, Luke faithfully recorded the details of the school match into his notebook. This time he used red ink rather than the usual black. Personal appearances always deserved to stand out. He made special mention of his vital role in both defence and attack.

He then switched on the computer to prepare for the Swifts' home league game the following afternoon. In the wake of Tubs's injury, the innovative coach wanted to devise a different team formation with adventurous, new tactics.

Instructions and diagrams filled several pages on the screen and churned out of the printer on to the floor.

Luke was in his element. Immersed in his own planning, with the radio blaring out a live match commentary and the latest football scores, he didn't even hear the calls to go down for his tea. Some things were more important than food.

He was up early next day, delivering the print-outs to his team members around the village so they'd have a chance to digest their contents before the game. He didn't bother calling on

Brain. Their star winger was severely dyslexic. Brain could read a pass far better than any words.

A quarter of an hour before kick-off, his team-mates were still poring over the pages in the changing cabin when Brain arrived late. 'Hello, what's all that?' he asked.

'Skip's latest world-beating schemes,' Dazza grinned. 'Haven't you got yours yet?'

Brain shook his head. 'He knows it'd be a waste of time giving them to me.'

'Lucky you!' laughed Gary.

'Lucky you, you mean, Gary,' said Luke. 'You're one of my new wing-backs. Just think of all that great attacking you'll be able to do up the left side!'

'Yeah, and all that slogging back again when some idiot goes and loses the ball,' he replied, deliberately catching Luke's eye.

'That's worrying me a bit too, Skip,' Dazza admitted. 'If you're expecting me to keep running back to help in defence, I'll be too knackered to do any real attacking.'

Luke brushed aside his misgivings. 'Rubbish! You'll love it, always being involved in the game. A lot of teams are using this system now – a three-man defence, with wing-backs to support

the midfield and attack.'

'You didn't dream all this guff up then?' said Big Ben, chucking his papers on to the floor.

Luke gathered them up and collected everyone else's too so they wouldn't deliberately lose them. He'd dish them out again for discussion at the next practice. 'Of course I didn't dream it,' he defended himself. 'When I played for the Comp yesterday at full-back and on the wing, I saw how easily you could combine the two positions.'

Tubs was leaning against the cabin wall. 'Glad I'm just watching today. Running's not for me. I can barely even walk at the moment.'

'Nobody would notice any difference,' Sanjay joked.

The grin was soon wiped off the goalkeeper's face. The ambitious changes proved disastrous, the players unable to cope with the demands of the system. Far from having just three men at the back, they could have done with about a dozen. Sanjay lost count of the number of times he picked the ball out the back of the net. In the end, he didn't even like to ask what the score was.

The Swifts sat around on the benches for a while afterwards, shell-shocked and exhausted, lacking the energy to start getting dressed.

'Back to the drawing-board, I reckon, Skipper,' said Brain.

Luke let out a loud sigh. 'Bound to be a few teething problems at first. Nothing we can't sort out in training. The tactics just need a bit of fine tuning, that's all.'

'Fine tuning!' Big Ben scoffed. 'They need a sledgehammer taken to them, if you ask me, and then thrown on the dump!'

'I reckon that mongrel had the best idea what to do with those print-outs,' observed Tubs, smirking. 'I think it's called passing an opinion!'

They burst out laughing, recalling the hilarious half-time incident. It would take some forgetting. Luke was in the middle of his team-talk, desperately attempting to salvage something from the wreckage, when a stray dog wandered up to their base-camp. It sniffed around their chewed slices of orange, then cocked its leg and piddled all over the pile of papers.

The look on the skipper's face was classic. For once, he'd been totally at a loss for words, his mouth still working, but with no sound coming out. As the Swifts fell about, the opposition had gazed across from their own camp in puzzlement. They couldn't fathom how a team that was

losing so heavily seemed to be having so much fun.

Swillsby Swifts had two more league matches to play before the third-round tie, the second of which was away to their cup opponents, Brenton Blues.

Luke was determined to persevere with his new strategies, sure that they would help to bring the best out of the players – eventually. 'If at first you don't succeed . . .' he murmured, wondering whether that was part of Kipling's poem as well. He couldn't quite remember. He knew he'd heard it somewhere before.

He was in front of the computer again, revising the plans before reprinting them. Nobody fancied having the original papers back.

'I shouldn't have tried to rush things through like that,' Luke mused, admitting – at least to himself – that he might have made a mistake. 'They couldn't take it all in at once.'

He broke off to study a tape of England's 4–1 thrashing of the Dutch at Wembley during Euro '96. It was Luke's favourite viewing. He'd watched it over and over again, analysing and admiring England's style of play. If Cruyff was Luke's footballing hero, then Terry Venables,

the England coach at the time, was his tactical genius.

'It's all about having the right players for the right jobs,' Luke said aloud to himself, returning to tinker with his formation further on the computer. 'Trouble is, I've got the right jobs, but the wrong players.'

Christmas was fast approaching and unless he could sign any new faces before the League's end-of-year transfer deadline, Luke knew that he'd have to make do with what he'd already got. He knuckled down to his task and at the Swifts' next training session, he presented everybody, including Brain, with a fresh batch of print-outs.

'You're serious about this, aren't you?' said Big Ben, leafing through them wearily. 'You're not going to give up.'

'Dead right!' Luke beamed. 'What's good enough for England is good enough for us.'

'I should point out,' said Mark, Big Ben's usual partner in the centre of defence, 'that international players are a little better than us.'

'C'mon, let's humour him,' sighed Big Ben. 'We'll give it another go.'

To their credit, the Swifts worked as hard as Luke could remember, but there was a limit to what they could achieve in practice. The true

test of their progress would be provided by the opposition on Sunday.

When that day came, a generous examiner might have given the Swifts six out of ten for effort. They did manage to match the England score, albeit in reverse, but there the similarity ended.

Luke and Brain – in theory – played behind Gregg as the main striker, but wing-backs Gary and Dazza were too often caught out of position. Luke couldn't really complain. After all, he only found himself where he should be by accident. Carried away by the excitement of the game, the skipper scoured the pitch, as always, rarely to be seen very far from the ball.

'Oh well, not too bad, I guess,' he reflected ruefully, bringing his Swifts' record book up to date later. 'Only lost four-one this time.'

At least his team had proved to themselves that the system might be made to work. They'd created more chances than usual and Dazza's strike near the end, sprinting on to Gary's cross to lash home a beauty, rewarded the Swifts with more than a mere consolation goal. It offered hope!

The next two games, in both league and cup, were now against the Blues and Luke kept

repeating his main message to the players in training. 'If we can't outplay 'em, we'll outnumber 'em,' he stressed, quoting Venables's guiding motto. 'We must try and get more of our men around the ball than theirs, especially in midfield.'

'We need extra help at the back as well, though,' Mark said. 'We can't afford to get overrun there like we were in the last match at times.'

'Point taken,' Luke conceded, 'but if we can win more of the ball in midfield, they won't be able to put our goal under pressure so much. Attack is the best form of defence!'

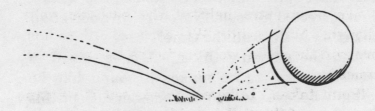

7   Christmas Tree

Brenton Blues were yo-yoing up and down in mid-table week by week, their inconsistency making them as likely to lose as to win games. It was also sufficient to give Luke genuine cause for optimism.

'With a bit of luck, we might just catch them on an off day,' he said brightly on the way to Brenton.

'Huh! With a lot of luck, more like,' grunted Sanjay.

'With a *lot* of luck, they might even have two off days,' Titch grinned. 'Today and in the cup next Sunday!'

'It's crucial we play well today, anyway,' Luke stressed. 'We need the points more than they do, and a result here would give us the psychological edge for the cup-tie at home.'

Sanjay looked at his skipper almost pityingly. 'You don't half talk some rubbish,' he began, then corrected himself. 'No, sorry, you don't *half* talk it – you do it all the time!'

'And the amazing thing is,' Tubs joined in between guffaws, 'he makes it sound like he actually believes we're good enough to beat this lot.'

Luke glanced at his dad, but knew that he had to stick up for himself. 'We *are*!' he insisted gamely. 'And we'll be even better when you're fit to play again, Tubs. You've left a big hole in our team.'

Tubs wondered for a moment if Luke was trying to be funny, but he might have guessed that Sanjay would spot the chance. 'I think you mean a crater, don't you, Skipper?' the goal-keeper giggled.

If this league encounter was going to give any psychological advantage to either team, it was the Swifts that took the initiative. And it was their much abused player-manager who had the honour of putting them ahead.

78

Brain set up the goal. He could have netted it himself, dribbling clear into the penalty area, but he saw his skipper unmarked and unselfishly squared the ball across the goal-mouth. It was easier to score than miss, but Luke nearly performed the more difficult option.

Unfortunately, the pass rolled to Luke's left foot. Its main job in life was to save him from hopping along all the time, but now he had to put it to more glamorous use. He shaped to steer the ball over the line but lost his balance and began to topple backwards. The ball skidded from the top of his boot and dollied up into the net off the inside of the post.

Luke lay flat on his back, soaking up the rare moment of perfect bliss. He was so relieved, he almost forgot to do his much-rehearsed, choreographed goal celebration. Suddenly he leapt to his feet and went jigging about the area in a dance that resembled a hyperactive monkey at a rave party. His teammates kept a respectful, embarrassed distance, hoping other people wouldn't think they were with him.

'Ought to be locked up, that kid,' grumbled one of the older home supporters. 'He's off his rocker!'

Even Uncle Ray stopped filming. He didn't think it was something that ought to be shown to young children.

Luke soon sobered up. The Blues hit back within a minute, capitalizing on slack marking in the middle of the Swifts' defence. The back three stared at one another accusingly, preferring that to excusing their lapse either to the skipper or, even worse, to an unimpressed Sanjay.

'Can't be helped, we all make mistakes,' Luke reassured his defenders at half-time, hoping nobody would point out that he normally made more than most. He was just thankful he hadn't messed up the open goal. 'We're still level, and there's everything to play for in the second half.'

'Not if we go and gift them any more early Christmas presents like that equalizer,' grumbled Sanjay. 'We're lucky they haven't scored more already. I haven't got enough cover in front of me.'

Under pressure from others, too, Luke agreed to revert to a four-man defence. Gary was deployed to stay tight on the Blues' right-winger whose lively runs had caused them major problems in the first period. It seemed to do the trick. Gary did a good man-marking job on him,

keeping the winger much quieter for the rest of the game, and the Swifts succeeded in clinging on for a 1–1 draw.

Their survival was not without its scares, especially when Sanjay fumbled a shot near the end that bobbled out of his hands and rolled just wide of a post, but it was well deserved. At least the Swifts thought so. They changed after the match in high spirits.

'They're no great shakes, these Blues,' said Gregg, voicing the general opinion. 'I reckon we can take them all right next week.'

It was music to Luke's ears. His own confidence seemed to be rubbing off on some of his team and they were beginning to have more faith in their abilities. He felt it was the right moment to unveil his latest plans.

'Our formation needs to be more flexible in future,' he told them. 'We've proved today we can adjust things even during a game, depending on how the other team play. I think it's time to put up the *Christmas tree*!'

'Now I know he's finally cracked,' groaned Sanjay. 'He's gonna block up our goal with a Christmas tree.'

'Yeah, and put Tubs on top as the fairy!' hooted Gary.

Luke joined in the laughter. 'It's just the name of the system 'cos of its shape,' he explained. 'Terry Venables first came up with it. It's a 4–3–2–1 line-up, tapering something like a Christmas tree.'

'How does that help?' asked Brain.

'Well, it makes sure we've got good numbers in defence and midfield when we need them,' Luke enthused. 'And it also gives us a launch-pad for our own attacks.'

'Just listen to him,' smiled Titch. 'He's off again!'

Luke spent part of the week trying to drum up more local support for the Swifts' big cup-tie on the recreation ground. He printed a dozen notices, using computer graphics, and put them on trees and walls around the village. He also pinned a few up in the school corridors.

The ones at the Comp were torn down as soon as Luke turned his back. Matthew even snatched a poster out of his hand and ripped it to pieces in front of him. 'That's what I think of the Sloths,' he snarled, choosing to ignore the fact that his own Panthers had suffered a shock, first-round knock-out by the Swifts. 'Just rubbish to chuck in the bin.'

Luke's efforts, however, had not been wasted. Quite a number of people began to gather on the touchline before the kick-off, even if over half of them, he realized, were Blues' supporters. He was delighted to see some parents and school-mates who had never previously turned up to watch.

'Attracted a crowd,' Gary observed from the changing-room door. 'I hope they haven't all come just to laugh at us.'

'Yeah, it wasn't so bad getting thrashed in private,' said Tubs, 'but I don't fancy being humiliated in public!'

Luke used the spectators as extra motivation for his team before they left the cabin. 'C'mon, men. We don't want to let our fans down. Let's show them how the Swifts can really play.'

'*Fans*, he calls them! He'll be wanting to start up a Swifts' fan club next!' chuckled Tubs, fit enough now to be named as their one and only sub. He was trying not to let it show how keen he was to play and sneaked a quiet word with Luke. 'You'll make sure I come on, won't you, Skipper? Half-time, maybe?'

'Can't promise, Tubs,' he replied. 'But I won't forget you, don't worry. Nice to have you back. We've missed you.'

'No kidding?' He grinned inanely at the flattery.

'Sure. We've had no-one to roll out the bumps on the pitch!'

Luke had to duck out the way of Tubs's playful swipe and then prepared to address his team. Sanjay beat him to it. 'Right, men. All ready?' the goalkeeper cried out.

'I say that!' Luke demanded above the laughter and then grinned. 'OK, c'mon, then. Let's get out there and light up that Christmas tree!'

It was a strange sort of game. It had to be strange when the Swifts had possession of the

ball more than their opponents. That phenomenon had never happened before. The new-look formation, worked on only in Saturday's practice session, denied Brenton space to play their football. The Blues' attacks were crowded out and once they'd broken down, the visitors often didn't find it easy to get the ball back again.

Luke was 'over the moon', as his commentary-jargon would no doubt say. There was no escaping his pitch-wide coverage. It was picked up on all wavelengths as he chased about like an over-excited puppy.

'Swifts are really turning on the style today! They're not letting the Blues settle on the ball and keep putting together slick passing moves of their own. Here's another one now as Dazza eats up the ground down the right, taking the ball out wide to stretch the Blues' shaky back-line yet again. Gregg, Brain and skipper Luke Crawford are waiting in the middle for the cross and over it comes . . . GOOOAAALLL!!!'

It wasn't exactly 'Goal of the Season', but it gave the Swifts a morale-boosting, half-time lead just the same. Gregg mistimed his header, Luke swung at the loose ball and missed, accidentally selling a dummy to two defenders, and

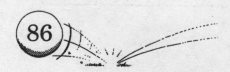

86

there was Brain lurking behind him to tuck it coolly into the net.

The Blues woke up to the dangers of defeat after the interval and pressed hard, but the Swifts' four-man defence looked more secure. To say the Christmas tree held its shape would be an exaggeration, but at least it stayed upright and didn't collapse.

The equalizer came as a bitter blow. It was stabbed home during a frantic goalmouth scramble, and for a while the visitors gained the upper hand, striving for the winner. Luke brought on Tubs as a panic measure to reinforce their midfield barrier, but it turned out to be an unintentional masterstroke.

With the tie heading towards another 1–1 stalemate and a replay back at Brenton, Tubs latched on to a clearance from Gary. He was a long way out from goal, too far to attempt going on a run – or waddle in his case – so he wound himself up and walloped the ball instead.

It was hit and hope. It was pain and ecstasy. The pain came from an immediate pull in the groin. The ecstasy came from seeing the ball thunder past the keeper's despairing dive as Tubs crumpled to the ground.

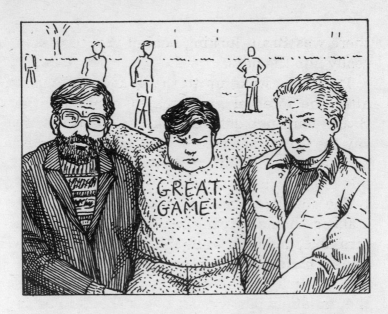

The hero had to be carried off the pitch by Luke's dad and uncle, which left the ten-man Christmas tree, shorn of its thickest branch, to withstand a raging storm. Somehow it did. The final whistle never sounded so sweet.

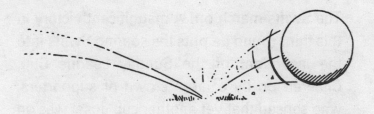

8   Foreign Signing

In his darkened bedroom that evening, Luke basked in the reflected glory of the computer screen's green light. He was drafting his regular match report for the sports page of Uncle Ray's monthly newspaper, the *Swillsby Chronicle*. No creative task gave him more pleasure, fuelling his ambitions one day to be a top soccer reporter. He gazed dreamily at his bold headline and then let the words flow from the keyboard.

CUP GIANT-KILLERS

by our soccer correspondent

Swillsby Swifts 2 – 1 Brenton Blues

The Swifts march on! A magnificent victory in this third round tie puts the soaring Swifts into the last eight of the Sunday League Cup. Cheered on by a large crowd of supporters, who sensed that yet another cup upset was on the cards, Swillsby played with an adventurous, attacking spirit that rocked the visitors. This was the second successive meeting between the two sides, but coach Luke Crawford had modified the Swifts' tactical system since their 1–1 draw in the league. Their new 'Christmas Tree' formation was designed to ensure there would be no gift goals for the Blues. 'Our best performance of the season so far,' said Luke later. 'The boys really played as a team.'

Brian 'Brain' Draper had put the Swifts ahead

by half-time, but when the Blues equalized the game seemed doomed for a replay. Player-manager Luke, however, still had one ace up his sleeve. He brought supersub Anthony 'Tubs' Tompson off the bench to produce the killer punch. Returning from injury, Tubs was hurt again as he blasted the ball home for the winning goal. 'It was worth the pain,' the scorer grinned afterwards. 'I just hope I'm fit for the quarter-finals.'

Skipper Luke is looking even beyond that. 'With a bit of luck,' he said, 'we're hoping this cup run leads all the way to the Final. This could be our year!'

When the *Chronicle* appeared the following week, just before the end of term, Tubs flourished a copy under Luke's nose. 'You've made me sound like a moron,' he protested. 'I didn't say nothing of the sort.'

'You might have done,' said Luke. 'It's called journalistic licence. It lets you put things in your report that maybe aren't strictly accurate. Don't you want to play in the next round, then?'

'Of course I do.'

93

'Well, then, what's all the fuss about? You got your name in the paper, didn't you?'

'Yeah, and that's another thing,' Tubs said, pulling a face. 'You spelt it all wrong. It's Antony without the "h" and Thompson with one!'

'Soz, I only know you as Tubs,' Luke grinned. 'Anyway, you've got plenty of time to get fit. The quarter-final game is our first one of the New Year, so go easy on the mince pies at Christmas.'

'Cut down on my food!' exclaimed Tubs. 'No fear! I'd rather be fat than fit!'

The Christmas holidays passed far too slowly for Luke.

With no real soccer action, apart from a few kickabouts with Jon in the back garden or with their mates on the recky, he felt at a loose end most of the time. He'd read all his new football annuals by Boxing Day.

Things only returned to normal when he had his Swifts report back for training on the Friday morning after New Year's Day. Luke was so excited about Sunday's big match, he was finding it hard to get to sleep. And he could barely wait to see the players' faces when he revealed his last-minute new signing!

They were going to need as much extra help as possible. Their quarter-final opponents were as tough as they come. The Swifts had been drawn away to Ridgeway Rovers, one of the top first division sides. Luke had wanted to have a good work out with the team and put them through their paces, but his plans were already in jeopardy.

He'd fully expected that the Christmas tree was bound to need a bit of sprucing up after the holidays, but he hadn't anticipated that two vital parts of it would have dropped off. The Garner twins were missing.

'Where are Gary and Gregg?' asked Titch, checking around the cabin as the squad changed into tracksuits. The weather was bitterly cold.

Luke frowned. 'They went up to Scotland to celebrate the New Year with relatives. They're not due back till tomorrow evening.'

'Cutting it a bit fine, isn't it?'

'It's about as welcome as your next-door neighbour learning to play the bagpipes,' Luke muttered. 'Nothing I can do about it, though. Their dad promised they'd be home in time for the game.'

'So long as they don't get snowed in up there,' Mark put in. 'It'd be goodbye cup dreams, if they weren't here.'

'Have you got any more dreams to tell us about, Skipper?' grinned Sean. He was the left-side, middle branch of their Christmas tree, the one with most of the fancy decorations on it. His be-ringed fingers were polishing his boots now to bring up the shine.

Luke shook his head. 'Haven't even had *that* one again since.'

'What about New Year resolutions, then?' Sanjay smiled. 'Made any of them? Like not inventing new tactics every week, for instance.'

'Yeah, and writing no more match reports,'

Tubs suggested.

'Actually, I have made one,' Luke said, cheering up. 'And it concerns all of us.'

'Thought it would do,' Big Ben groaned. 'C'mon, let's hear it.'

'Yeah, the sooner we know what it is, the sooner we can break it,' laughed Tubs. 'Mine didn't last five minutes.'

'What was it?'

'Resolved to lose weight by not eating chocolate. And then I just had to have a caramel bar to console myself! Soz, Skipper!'

'We'll have to get the cabin door widened for you,' Luke said pointedly. 'Anyway, do you want me to tell you or not?'

'Anything to stay in here a bit longer,' said Sanjay to murmurs of agreement. The cabin was draughty, but it was better than being outside. For once, they were happy to let Luke talk as much as he liked.

'Your skipper has firmly resolved that the Swifts will do the Double!' he proclaimed. 'Win the cup and also escape relegation!'

The wooden cabin almost collapsed with the roars of laughter and stamping of boots on bare boards. Luke waited for the rumpus to die down.

'I'm deadly serious, team. And I know just the

97

guy who's gonna help us do it. My cousin!'

'Jon!' Mark gasped. 'Have you gone and signed Jon up for the Swifts?'

'He's cup-tied,' said Big Ben. 'Played for the Panthers, remember.'

Luke's grin was as wide as the Cheshire cat's. 'No, this isn't Jon. He's a cousin of ours who only arrived in this country over Christmas. The Swifts now boast the League's first Italian import!'

The Swifts were all agog to see their new player. Luke banged twice on the partition wall as a signal and through the adjoining door from the visitors' changing room appeared a tall, athletic-looking figure.

'This is Ricki,' Luke announced. 'Ricki, meet your new teammates.'

Tubs's jaw dropped. 'You're not another Crawford, are you?'

Ricki smiled and shook his head. 'You have plenty Crawfords already,' he said with a strong accent. 'My full name is Ricardo Fortuna.'

'My aunt married an Italian,' Luke explained. 'They've come to live in England for a while so I snapped him up. Just got the registration forms completed before the transfer deadline.'

'Fantastic!' said Sanjay with genuine enthusiasm. 'Are you gonna play for the Comp too?'

Ricki looked puzzled and Luke answered for him. 'Ricki's going to Padley High School, I'm afraid. Old Frosty won't be able to get his hands on him, but he'll be playing for us as often as he can.'

'Not every week?' said Brain, disappointed.

'I am sorry,' said Ricki. 'We love rugby in our family too. Rugby is plenty big sport in Italy now.'

'So when he's not playing rugby, he'll turn out for us,' said Luke. 'Starting with the cup match on Sunday!'

'With a name like Fortuna, he's got to bring us good luck,' laughed Dazza. 'And we're sure gonna need loadsa luck against Rovers.'

'Too right. Rovers are in a different league to us,' said Titch.

'Yeah, three leagues higher,' Mark grinned. 'Perhaps we should challenge them to a game of rugby instead.'

'Good idea!' said Tubs. 'I'm better at rugby. I've got the right build for that.'

Sanjay smirked at him. 'You're the size of a whole scrum on your own.'

'What position do you play in, Ricki?' asked Sean.

'In the centre. But I like to score tries too.'

'Luke just tries to score,' Tubs chuckled, wondering if Ricki knew what he was letting himself in for. 'Has he shown you the league table?'

'I've told him we're in a false position,' Luke said quickly. 'With Ricki in the team, things can only get better. He's incredibly fit from doing all his sport in Italy.'

If Ricki was not yet aware of the Swifts' standard of football, the lack of knowledge was mutual. One thing Luke didn't care to admit to his team was that he hadn't even seen his Italian cousin play.

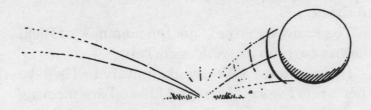

9 Happy New Year?

The Swifts were still talking about Ricki as they drove to the match. His performance at Friday's practice had been patchy – part Jon, part Luke.

'I don't like to say this, but I'm not too sure he's really up to much,' said Mark. 'Seemed to think he was playing rugby half the time, the way he kept catching the ball.'

'Perhaps it was too cold for him,' said Big Ben. 'He's not used to our winter weather yet.'

'Well, let's hope he'll feel more at home playing Rovers,' Mark sighed. 'They're red-hot favourites to win the cup.'

Luke was pleased with the size of the convoy heading for Ridgeway Park in Padley. Five cars trailed behind his dad's, but how he wished there'd been another. Mr Garner had failed to show up at the usual meeting point and the Garner house was empty when they went there to check.

'You know we've only got ten men now, if Ricki doesn't turn up as well,' said Tubs.

'I can count,' Luke said, irritated. 'He'll be there, don't worry. Him and his dad are meeting us at the park. They live right next to it.'

To Luke's undisguised relief, Ricki was already waiting for them near the changing pavilion. He had a rugby ball tucked under his arm.

'What have you got that for?' Luke asked. 'It's football today.'

Ricki grinned. 'Dad always gives me plenty practice with kicking.'

'Just remember, Ricki,' Tubs began, miming the shape of a round ball. 'In soccer, we try and kick the ball under the crossbar, not over it!'

Ricki laughed. 'I like you, Tubs. You make plenty good jokes, yes? We all good jokers here.'

'Yeah, that's right, Ricki, you catch on quick,' he replied. 'The Swifts are plenty big joke!'

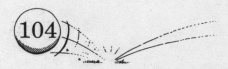

104

There was still no sign of Gary and Gregg by kick-off time and Luke desperately rearranged his line-up to cover for their absence. He didn't even attempt to explain to Ricki about their Christmas tree.

'Just put yourself about plenty,' he instructed his cousin, picking up Ricki's favourite word as well. 'Up and down the pitch, all over, winning the ball. Prove how fit you are. *Comprendo*? Got it?'

'Got it!' he said with a grin, sticking his thumb up. 'No worries.'

Sadly, Luke soon had many things to worry about. Rovers scorched into a 2–0 lead without

even breaking sweat. The first goal came by courtesy of Sean's careless back-pass, finding a Rovers' attacker instead of Sanjay, and the second was a penalty.

Ricki's flying tackle had the desired effect of making the opponent lose control of the ball, but his chosen method wasn't to be found in any soccer coaching manual. He'd dived full-length and wrapped his arms around the boy's ankles to bring him crashing down.

'I am plenty sorry, Skipper,' he said sheepishly after the referee had booked him for the foul. 'I forget.'

Luke sighed. 'Just don't do it again, OK? You were lucky you didn't get yourself sent off.'

The Swifts' supporters on the touchline shuffled their feet. 'I have a terrible feeling this might get very embarrassing,' muttered Luke's dad.

'Didn't help when our brother-in-law applauded Ricki's tackle,' said Ray. 'He'll be wanting him to dive over the line for a try next!'

Jon was with them. The Panthers had no match arranged and he'd come along to cheer his cousins on. 'Ricki's bound to be nervous at first,' he said charitably. 'You wait until he settles down. I reckon he can play a bit. He looked good taking shots at Sanjay in the warm-up.'

'Anybody can look good shooting at Sanjay!' his dad chuckled. 'We want to see him troubling the keeper at the other end.'

As they spoke, a defender wandered idly up to Tubs who was playing in Gregg's role as lone striker at the top of the tree. 'This is gonna be a massacre. How did you lot manage to get as far as these quarter-finals?'

Tubs shrugged his bulky shoulders. 'I think it's called being fluky.'

'Well I reckon your luck's finally run out,' the boy sniggered.

'Don't count on it,' smiled Tubs as they both heard Luke coming towards them. 'Our captain probably thinks Johan Cruyff will suddenly come on as sub to rescue us!'

Luke's rambling commentary did seem to be clutching at straws. *The Swifts are not giving up hope yet. Player-manager Luke Crawford's boys are made of sterner stuff nowadays and don't expect to lose games like they used to. They know it only takes one kick to score a goal, and that would put them right back in it. And the Garner twins may yet arrive . . .*

He broke off. He could scarcely believe his eyes. For a moment, he thought Jon had nipped on to the pitch and gone swooping down the wing with the ball, but then he realized it was cousin Ricki instead. Luke hared off in pursuit, as did Tubs more slowly, but Ricki clearly needed no support.

For a tall lad, he had lightning feet and his body swerves at speed left two baffled Rovers trailing in his wake. As the goalie advanced, Ricki unleashed a rasping shot in his stride from outside the box. The ball curled and dipped and struck the crossbar with a crack that might have echoed over to Italy and back.

'Magic!' cried Dazza. 'That's showed 'em we

mean business.'

'Keep tighter on that big kid,' shouted the Rovers' captain. 'We can't give him room to run at us like that again. He's deadly!'

Ricki's blast out of the blue set the game alight, firing up his own team's flagging spirits and earning the Swifts new respect from their opponents. In one flash of inspiration, he had achieved more than Luke could ever dream of doing. The skipper had to be content with his decision to take the risk of signing his cousin up into Swifts' colours before it was too late.

'That might be the turning point of the Swifts' season,' he told his imagined host of listeners as well as any players nearby. *'Whatever happens in this match, the future looks brighter. The Christmas tree now has a real glittering star!'*

The cup-tie became a more even contest for a time as the Swifts fought fiercely for control of the midfield and enjoyed their fair share of the ball. Rovers were made to work much harder than they'd anticipated, struggling to find a path through the tree's maze of tangled branches. When they finally did so, their third goal brought the first division side very welcome extra breathing space at the interval.

'This is more like it,' Luke praised his team as

they huddled together, quite pleased with themselves, despite the 3–0 scoreline. 'We've not lost yet. Keep it up. All we need is . . .'

Jon came running up to interrupt. 'The Garners are here. Look!'

'Think I must have a bang on the head,' said Ricki, shaking it. 'I am seeing double!'

'It's OK, Ricki,' laughed Sean. 'It's only the twins.'

'Happy New Year, guys,' Tubs welcomed them as they raced from the car to join the group. ''Fraid the party's nearly over, though.'

'Soz, Skipper,' gasped Gregg. 'Car broke down. Had all sorts of problems getting home.'

'Got trouble here too, I gather,' said Gary.

'Not as bad as we thought at first, thanks to Ricki,' grinned Dazza.

'Who?' they chorused.

'It's a long story,' said Luke. 'Just go and get your gear on quick, both of you – at the double!'

The Swifts' Little and Large pairing of Titch and Tubs were the unlucky ones to make way, and Ricki immediately introduced himself to the twin substitutes in spectacular style.

Brain sent a head-high cross into the Rovers' penalty area and Ricki met it with an acrobatic bicycle-kick. It took everyone by surprise.

111

Mesmerized by the whirling limbs, the keeper never moved a muscle as Ricki made perfect contact and the ball zipped past him into the net.

It was a stunning goal. And before Rovers could recover, their lead was reduced even further. Luke accepted a pass from Ricki on the edge of the area, thought about having a shot himself, but wisely ruled it out and toe-poked the ball forward instead to set Gregg up for a simple second.

Against any other side, the Swifts might perhaps have gone on to win. They were playing well enough to cause such a shock. But Ridgeway Rovers were just too good a team to let that happen. Encouraged by their large home support, the Rovers managed to weather the storm and regain their grip on the game – mainly by trying to keep Ricki out of it.

The Rovers were also fitter than the Swifts. Although Ricki was still charging around, the others were feeling the strain. The great comeback had taken a heavy toll on their energies and as they tired, gaps opened up in the team's defences and Rovers helped themselves to two more late goals.

Luke's weary commentary attempted to sum up their looming 5–2 defeat philosophically.

'End of the road for the Swifts in the cup. End of a dream, too – but there's always next year. Football's all about winning and losing. You have to learn to accept both. You can't win 'em all, as they say . . .'

Brain overheard him. 'Never mind, Skipper. At least we're starting to win *some*. Shows we must be getting better.'

'Bang goes my New Year resolution, though,' Luke sighed.

'One out of two ain't so bad,' the winger grinned.

Luke brightened up. 'That's true. Now we're out the cup, we can concentrate on the league. We've still got a relegation battle to win!'

The skipper found some comfort again in Kipling's famous lines:

'If you can dream – and not make dreams
your master,
If you can think – and not make thoughts
your aim,
If you can meet with Triumph and Disaster,
And treat those two impostors just the same,
You'll be a man, my son!'

He felt his players had all grown up a bit after

such a performance – especially in self-respect and confidence. Luke looked at them proudly as the final whistle blew. They were exhausted, but still smiling in defeat. They knew they'd given it their best shot. And that was a kind of triumph.

'Nobody will be able to call us Luke's Flukes any more now,' he murmured in satisfaction.

THE END

CRAWFORD'S CORNER

Hi! Luke here. They've let me have a few pages of my own at last – and about time too! All footballers need a bit of space to really express themselves. Oops! Just split an infinitive there. 'Do I not like that!' as my English teacher might say sarcastically. (She knows I plan to be a commentator and soccer journalist when my playing career is over.)

Anyway, what they want me to do is write about the different team formations that I devised for the Swifts in this book. Hope you enjoyed it, by the way. We were dead unlucky in the end, don't you think? Still, that's football. It's a funny old game, as the saying goes.

Glad to have the chance to tell you more about it all. You might even like to try out a couple of these formations in the teams you play for. (Of course, it helps if you're the skipper, player-manager and

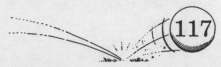

coach, too, like me, otherwise the Boss – or perhaps the teacher – might get narked if you start re-organizing the players without consulting them.) Failing that, you could always practise with your Subbuteo teams. Baffle your opponents with your cunning, new line-up!

While I'm on the subject, I thought I'd also go into the history of the way formations have developed over the years. I've been consulting my footie reference books and it's dead interesting. Well, at least I think so. I'm not called a walking soccer encyclopedia for nothing, you know.

Nowadays on TV, you'll hear the pundits ranting on about 4-4-2, 4-2-4, 4-3-3 and 3-5-2 formations, flat back fours, sweepers, split strikers, wing-backs and even the Christmas Tree. They can't always fit the various patterns on to the screen properly when they show the teams – and even then it's often calculated guesswork, trying to read the manager's mind.

For most of the twentieth century, however, up till about the 1950s, every team played with the same system. It's known as the WM formation because if you joined up the dots between the

players on paper, so to speak, you could make those letters. They always wore numbers from 1 to 11, too, not 35 or whatever that huge squads have today. Numbers really meant something then. They told you the player's exact position on the pitch, some of them unheard of now, and even the kind of player he was.

Wingers were usually small, nippy dribblers, hugging the touchline; inside-forwards tended to be skilful ball players; wing-halves were rugged, hard tackling men with cannonball shots; full-backs stayed in their own half, kicked the winger into the crowd and hoofed the ball upfield; centre-forwards were big, brave, powerful men who could run through a brick wall; and centre-halves were built with tree trunks for legs and with necks just as thick for heading the old, heavy, leather footballs.

As for the goalkeepers, they were *well* crazy in those days. They had to be. Few of them still had their own teeth, but collected those of centre-forwards instead when their punch missed the ball. It was too risky to try and catch it. They'd get barged into the net along with the ball!

Teams would line up like this in that WM shape:

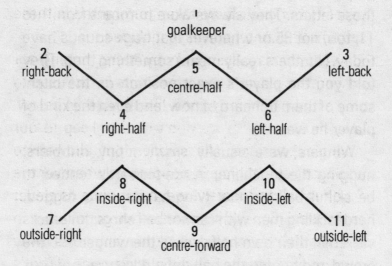

```
                    1
                goalkeeper

  2                                         3
right-back          5                    left-back
                centre-half

      4                            6
  right-half                    left-half


      8                           10
  inside-right                inside-left
  7                   9                    11
outside-right   centre-forward         outside-left
```

The wing-halves (defenders) and inside-forwards (attackers) were sort of midfield men, but the term hadn't been invented then. Midfielders only came into existence as teams began to experiment with more imaginative line-ups. The legendary Brazilians, with Pele in his famous number ten shirt, won the World Cup in 1958 and 1962 using the 4-2-4 arrangement. They weren't playing with only ten men of course – although this

lot might well have been able to win without a keeper – but goalies are taken for granted in these systems and aren't normally included.

Other teams began to copy them, hoping for similar success, and Swillsby Swifts in fact used to play a loose 4-2-4 formation, like the line-up below. I say loose because we don't tend to keep to our intended positions. (As skipper, I'm allowed to wander all over the pitch, popping up wherever the action is.) Unfortunately, we're not quite as clever as the Brazilians and all too often we got overrun in midfield. That meant we gave too many goals away because our defence just couldn't cope. (That's another way of saying that they weren't good enough to keep the ball out of our net, but don't tell them I said that!)

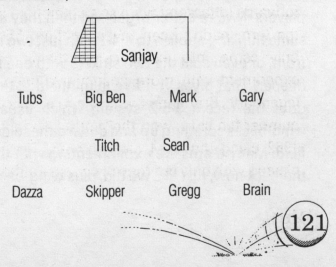

Sanjay

Tubs   Big Ben   Mark   Gary

Titch   Sean

Dazza   Skipper   Gregg   Brain

121

Then in 1966, Alf Ramsey came up with 4-3-3 to win the World Cup for England in the Geoff Hurst hat-trick final at Wembley (see this story for more exciting details). He only used this style of play as he reckoned he hadn't got any decent wingers so his team were called the Wingless Wonders. What that did, apart from earning Sir Alf a knighthood, was show that managers need to adapt their tactics to suit their own players – or to deal with the strengths and weaknesses of the opposition.

After that, playing 4-3-3 became more fashionable because managers realized you had a greater chance of dominating a game by putting an extra player in midfield. The theory is that if you can't outplay 'em, outnumber 'em! That way, even the Swifts can possibly beat a team with more talented players if we're better organized than they are. The same thinking applies to 4-4-2 with just two men up front, or even split the two strikers with one playing deeper. That gives you five in midfield at times, as does the recent 3-5-2 system which usually has wing-backs sprinting up and down either side of the field. Many teams are experimenting with three-at-the-back now, just like we did, plus wing-backs who

have that double job to do.

In the Euro '96 Championships, the England coach, Terry Venables, came so close to glory by boldly choosing attack-minded wingers as sort of wing-backs instead of defenders. He also invented the Christmas Tree, a formation that tapers to the front of the team, 4-3-2-1, like the shape of the traditional pine tree. It's a flexible system, giving you plenty of men around the ball in midfield and lots of attacking options too.

Just imagine this as a dream team, using the Christmas Tree: (I've stood the tree up the right way, using the goalie as the plant pot!)

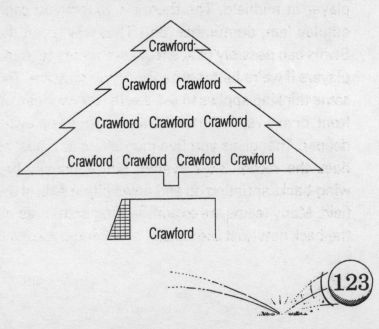

A team like that – with a bit of luck – could take on the world! Only dreaming, sadly. If only I was as good a player as cousin Jon. IF . . . Now that's a very big word. It's all right knowing the theory – it's doing it on the pitch I find so tricky. Just have to keep working on those skills.

See you again soon, I hope. Enjoy your footie!

Luke

ABOUT THE AUTHOR

Rob Childs was born and grew up in Derby. His childhood ambition was to become an England cricketer or footballer – preferably both! After university, however, he went into teaching and taught in primary and high schools in Leicestershire, where he now lives. Always interested in school sports, he coached school teams and clubs across a range of sports, and he ran area representative teams in football, cricket and athletics.

Recognizing a need for sports fiction for young readers, he decided to have a go at writing such stories himself and now has more than thirty books to his name, including the popular *The Big Match* series, published by Young Corgi Books.

Rob now combines his writing career with work helping dyslexic students (both adults and children) to overcome their literacy difficulties. Married to Joy, also a writer, Rob has a "lassie" dog called Laddie and is also a keen photographer.

ROB CHILDS

ALL GOALIES ARE CRAZY

... BUT SOME ARE MORE CRAZY THAN OTHERS!

No-one enjoys keeping goal so much as Sanjay Mistry – the regular, if unpredictable, goalie both for the school team and Swillsby Swifts, the Sunday league team led by soccer-mad Luke Crawford. But after Sanjay makes a series of terrible match-losing blunders, Luke decides that it's time someone else had a go at playing in goal – himself!

Determined to prove himself as the number one goalie, Sanjay rises to the challenge with some outstanding and acrobatic saves. But Luke's enthusiasm and crazy antics make him a surprisingly serious rival . . .

A fast-moving and realistic football tale, the second in the *Soccer Mad* series.

0 440 863503

ROB CHILDS

SOCCER MAD

'This is going to be the match of the century!'

Luke Crawford is crazy about football. A walking encyclopedia of football facts and trivia, he throws his enthusiasm into being captain of the Swillsby Swifts, a Sunday team made up mostly of boys like himself – boys who love playing football but get few chances to play in real matches.

Luke is convinced that good teamwork and plenty of practice can turn his side into winners on the pitch, but he faces a real challenge when the Swifts are drawn to play the Padley Panthers – the league stars – in the first round of the Sunday League Cup . . .

The first title in an action-packed new football series.

0 440 863449